Little Esther was a friendly and happy girl, with a lot of smiles to share, and a great big love for God.

Esther loved her Uncle, Mordecai. He was like a father to her. Mordecai was a servant in the kings palace.

Little Esther loved to be out in nature, running, skipping and making flower crowns.

Mordecai taught her many things about God and God's people, the Jews.

Many years later, King Xerxes, the ruler of Persia, was looking for a wife. "Bring all the prettiest woman in the land to my palace, so I can meet them!" he said.

Esther had grown up to be a very beautiful woman. If she was chosen to be the queen, then Esther and Mordecai could miss each other.

King Xerxes found Esther to be the prettiest of them. He fell in love with her and chose her to be his queen.

It was amazing to be the queen. A new experience and a new life, but she was also sad to say good-bye to her Uncle, Mordecai.

One day, Mordecai heard some terrible news: A powerful man named Haman, tricked the king to agree to get rid of all the Jews.

Mordecai was so sad, that he ripped his clothes and put ashes on himself. Esther saw him from the window wondered, "What is wrong with my Uncle Mordecai? Is he sick?"

Esther sent her servant to find out. When Esther heard the news, she was also very sad. But what could she do? She was only a young woman.

"Esther must tell the king about Haman's evil plan!" Mordecia told the servant. "We must find a way to stop him."

But Esther was afraid. "I cannot go and see the king unless he calls for me. The law says I could even be put to death."

God gave Esther a plan. She put on her best clothes, she fixed her hair. And with great courage, she went to see the king.

The king was surprised to see her, "Why would she risk her life to come and see me without being called?" he wondered.

But she looked more beautiful than ever. The king raised his scepter to show that she was welcome.

And so Haman and the king enjoyed a wonderful meal. "Tell me, my queen, what would you like me to give to you?" the king asked.

The king wrote a new law that saved queen Esther and the Jews, God's people. So with God's help and courage, Esther brought peace to her people. God had allowed her to be queen for this very important time.

Esther, Mordecai and all of the Jews gave glory and praise to God.

They also thanked their brave and beautiful queen Esther.